On Natural Order: Philosophic Reflections on Right Libertarian Reality, in the Context of Theological Existence

Caenan Perez

Fulton Books
Meadville, PA

Published by Fulton Books 2024

ISBN 979-8-89221-032-4 (paperback)
ISBN 979-8-89221-033-1 (digital)

Printed in the United States of America

Contents

Reflection on the Philosophic System of Right Libertarian Reality

Libertarianism, as understood within the Rothbardian tradition, is a purely axiomatic-deductive theory. Libertarianism begins with axioms of human action and nature and deduces a system of economics, ethics, jurisprudence, and politics from those axioms; libertarianism is protophysical synthetic a priroi knowledge of reality[1]. In following axiomatic-deductive reasoning, the praxeological program of the Austrians will be adhered to. A priori true, without any observation or falsification, it is known that humans are individuals, humans have wants and needs, humans employ means to achieve ends. Humans are limited in nature, and have a diversity and verticality of talents, aptitudes, responsibilities, and inheritances. Subject to the universal phenomenon of the law of scarcity, humans must enter into the division of labor in order to produce and exchange goods and services that fulfill those ends of human actors. In order to communicate and measure value within the economic division of labor, persons agree to a common market media in the form of money and currency; this allows for one to communicate one's subjective valuation of titles of property to exchanging and producing human actors. Because production and exchange will need the accumulation of greater capital value over time, there must be economic integration of the division of labor in order to widen the scope of available scarce resource ready

---

[1] "Its statements and propositions are not derived from experience. They are, like those of logic and mathematics, a priori. They are not subject to verification and falsification on the ground of experience and facts. They are both logically and temporally antecedent to any comprehension of historical facts. They are a necessary requirement of any intellectual grasp of historical events."

to be employed in economic production. Thus, unrestricted free trade and contract must be recognized in order to achieve this much needed economic integration so as to allow more persons with praxeological goals to exchange and produce with each other. Persons acting within the division of labor will also organize themselves in accordance with not only their marginal utility, but their time preference; those that seek out the accumulation of greater value in their capital (capitalists) will delay gratification by investing into greater capital and paying out wages to laborers to invest their labor into this capitalist actor's good for the aforementioned increase in value. In other words, the capitalist supplies the laborer with present goods in the form of wages, while the laborer supplies the capitalist with future goods. The demand of each of the human actors, then, has been appropriately supplied, the just market price of rates of interest has been determined. Economic production and exchange is underpinned by an epistemological-deontological ethical framework of natural property rights deduced from axioms of justice. Ethics deals with the normative ends that allows for adherence to those very economic laws. For this division of labor to emerge, there must be adherence to titles of property that were originally appropriated through the mixing of labor or the voluntary transfer of title. Collective ownership of property is a logical contradiction, and all factors of production should be economically privatized and liberalized, including production of defense and justice[2]. In Power and Market, Murray

---

[2] "…Rothbard first makes us aware of the following: for something to be an economic good at all, it must be scarce and must be realized as scarce by someone. In other words, something is not a good-as-such, but goods are goods only in the eyes of some beholder. But when goods are never goods-as-such, when no physicochemical analysis can establish something as an economic good, then there is also no fixed, objective criterion for classifying goods as public or private. They can never be private or public goods as such; their private or public character depends on how few or how many people consider them goods (or for that matter, bads), with the degree to which they are private or public changing as these evaluations change and ranging from 1 to infinity…even if all these difficulties were set aside, the conclusion reached by the public goods theorists is a glaring non sequitur, as Rothbard shows. For one thing, to come to the conclusion that the state has to provide public goods

Rothbard begins his chapter "Defense Services on the Free Market" with the observation that economists fail to recognize the normative claims of property rights that need to be accounted for in consistent economic theory. Since true economics deals with real people and their real relations, the nature of their rights must be considered as humans are not malleable objects subject to experimentation. There also must be a theory of justice that allows for the unleashing of economic laws by understanding and justifying the nature and right of property[3]. Economists then cannot ignore the normative ethics of the titles of property; one must assert that there is an ethical judgement regarding the arrangement of property titles among human actors, and that this arrangement of property titles is an objective moral reality. Rothbard sought a deontological libertarianism, based on the natural rights and the rational scholastic method, that constructs a rational system of ethics based on the principles of a priori private property rights and self-ownership[4]. Libertarianism forbids

---

that otherwise would not be produced, one must smuggle a norm into one's chain of reasoning. Otherwise, from the statement that because of some special characteristics certain goods would not be produced, one could never reach the conclusion that these goods should be produced. With a norm required to justify their conclusion, the public goods theorists clearly have left the bounds of economics as a positive science and transgressed the field of ethics. None of them, however, offers anything faintly resembling a clear system of ethics."

[3] "Thus, there has been general neglect of the fact that free exchange means exchange of titles of ownership to property, and that, therefore, the economist is obliged to inquire into the conditions and the nature of the property ownership that would obtain in the free society. If a free society means a world in which no one aggresses against the person or property of others, then this implies a society in which every man has the absolute right of property in his own self and in the previously unowned natural resources that he finds, transforms by his own labor, and then gives to or exchanges with others. A firm property right in one's own self and in the resources that one finds, transforms, and gives or exchanges, leads to the property structure that is found in free-market capitalism. Thus, an economist cannot fully analyze the exchange structure of the free market without setting forth the theory of property rights, of justice in property, that would have to obtain in a free-market society."

[4] Aquinas, then, realized that men always act purposively, but also went beyond this to argue that ends can also be apprehended by reason as either objectively good or bad for man. For Aquinas, then, in the words of Copleston, "there is

the initiation of force against person and property, and the only just

---

therefore room for the concept of 'right reason,' reason directing man's acts to the attainment of the objective good for man." Moral conduct is therefore conduct in accord with right reason: "If it is said that moral conduct is rational conduct, what is meant is that it is conduct in accordance with right reason, reason apprehending the objective good for man and dictating the means to its attainment." In natural-law philosophy, then, reason is not bound, as it is in modern post-Humean philosophy, to be a mere slave to the passions, confined to cranking out the discovery of the means to arbitrarily chosen ends. For the ends themselves are selected by the use of reason; and "right reason" dictates to man his proper ends as well as the means for their attainment. For the Thomist or natural-law theorist, the general law of morality for man is a special case of the system of natural law governing all entities of the world, each with its own nature and its own ends...Let us now return to our analysis of Crusoe's purposeful transformation of nature-given data though the understanding of natural laws. Crusoe finds virgin, unused land on the island; land, in short, unused and uncontrolled by anyone, and hence unowned. By finding land resources, by learning how to use them, and, in particular, by actually transforming them into a more useful shape, Crusoe has, in the memorable phrase of John Locke, "mixed his labor with the soil." In doing so, in stamping the imprint of his personality and his energy on the land, he has naturally converted the land and its fruits into his property. Hence, the isolated man owns what he uses and transforms; therefore, in his case there is no problem of what should be A's property as against B's. Any man's property is ipso facto what he produces, i-e., what he transforms into use by his own effort. His property in land and capital goods continues down the various stages of production, until Crusoe comes to own the consumer goods which he has produced, until they finally disappear through his consumption of them. As long as an individual remains isolated, then, there is no problem whatever about how far his property-his ownership-extends; as a rational being with free will, it extends over his own body, and it extends further over the material goods which he transforms with his labor. Suppose that Crusoe had landed not on a small island, but on a new and virgin continent, and that, standing on the shore, he had claimed "ownership" of the entire new continent by virtue of his prior discovery. This assertion would be sheer empty vainglory, so long as no one else came upon the continent. For the natural fact is that his true property, his actual control over material goods-would extend only so far as his actual labor brought them into production. His true ownership could not extend beyond the power of his own reach.9 Similarly, it would be empty and meaningless for Crusoe to trumpet that he does not "really" own some or all of what he has produced (perhaps this Crusoe happens to be a romantic opponent of the property concept), for in fact the use and therefore the ownership has already been his. Crusoe, in natural fact, owns

use of force is in defense of that very person and property subject to aggression. The arrangement of justice demanded by libertarianism must then not come from an artificial assortment of objects that does not exist but must be grounded in ethics derived from the relations that emerge from self-owning human actors; libertarianism, then, is a truth that exists independent of our minds and is grounded in a natural order in which man can know through reason. Libertarianism is protophysical synthetic a priori knowledge that comes first before any empircal investigation. Man's reason is the faculty in which we are able to arrive at ends and explain the nature of things; St. Aquinas asserted in his natural-law philosophy that moral conduct is rational conduct, and that the apprehension of the ethical and physical laws of the natural order must be by the faculty of reason[5]. The natural order is one that is objective and guides the ends of man through the determination of what is just and is unjust independent of his subjective value. Because of the nature of man having dominion over his reasoning powers and his bodily functions, and the universal fact of scarcity exists within the laws of the natural order, it is only right and just for one to have the apriori right to property as a presuppo-

---

his own self and the extension of his self into the material world, neither more nor less.

[5]   [T]he precepts of the natural law are to the practical reason, what the first principles of demonstrations are to the speculative reason; because both are self-evident principles…Now a certain order is to be found in those things that are apprehended universally. For that which, before aught else, falls under apprehension, is "being," the notion of which is included in all things whatsoever a man apprehends. Wherefore the first indemonstrable principle is that "the same thing cannot be affirmed and denied at the same time," which is based on the notion of "being" and "not-being…Now as "being" is the first thing that falls under the apprehension simply, so "good" is the first thing that falls under the apprehension of the practical reason, which is directed to action: since every agent acts for an end under the aspect of good. Consequently, the first principle of practical reason is one founded on the notion of good, viz. that "good is that which all things seek after." Hence this is the first precept of law, that "good is to be done and pursued, and evil is to be avoided." All other precepts of the natural law are based upon this: so that whatever the practical reason naturally apprehends as man's good (or evil) belongs to the precepts of the natural law as something to be done or avoided.

sition for apprehending rules that order one's actions in accordance with justice. However, this natural-law philosophy can indeed be strengthened, in particular against the fact-value dichotomy; natural-law philosophy is Hans-Hermann Hoppe sought out in the late 1980's to contribute an ultimate justification of the libertarian ethic through apriori argumentation; that is, the argumentation is an act of reason and conflict-free use of the scarce resource of the human body. Hoppe constructs argumentation as being predicated upon a set of norms. Argumentation implies universalizability, but it is an affair that is both an act of reasoning and practice, and argumentation is an act of using the scarce resources of one's body. When one sets out to argue, the implication within the act is that I have asserted in fact that I have ownership over my reasoning powers and bodily functions, as this was an act performed by myself.

And because argumentation is an act that is universally applicable to all humans, the further implication is that I ought to also recognize that those who argue also have ownership over their reasoning power and bodily functions. As an extension of this self-ownership, one must presuppose that there exists a theory of property in which humans, through original appropriation and title-transfer contract, can and must own property in order for argument to commence. Although the natural-law philosophy compels on to make value judgements, and while argumentation ethics is a value-free justification, both are realist in the understanding and can indeed be reconciled into an argumentative natural-law, or a natural rights theory based on argumentation. This philosophical synthesis can be referred to as right libertarianism, or transcendental realist libertarianism. The epistemological background of argumentation ethics is an Aristotelian realist interpretation of Kantianism; argumentation ethics seeks to establish the libertarian ethic as a synthetic a priori axiom, that can be definitively true through cognitive reflection upon the rights of the human person over their person and property. However, it is compatible with natural-law scholasticism in that this synthetic apriori can be directly known to rational beings, Indeed, the transcendental deduction of Kantian epistemology can indeed affirm the deontology of natural-law-natural rights, as dialectical reasoning is now a necessity of argumentation. The natural law-natural rights system is furthermore affirmed as existing within one's conscience, bound to reality through the bridge of human action, with argumentation ethics acting as the dialectally necessary presupposition of logical transcendental deduction. Thus, a radical construction of natural rights beginning with argumentation ethics will affirm absolutely the definitive synthetic a priori truth of one's rights and liberties, rather than being a product of relative empirical inquiry. Instead of artificial treaties, constitutions of natural rights are to be an integrated body of cognitive arguments within a reality of human action; since the laws of the libertarian natural order are independent of our mind, yet directly accessible through human action, just constitutions of law can only be from cognitive argument. This starkly contrasts against the empirical-material conception of law; that is, law is made, rather than arrived at through transcendent deduction from cognitive argument. With that being said, radical liberty derived from an integrated philosophic body that draws upon aprioristic laws of economics, natural rights, and argumentation, allows for one to deduce that the only justified economic, jurisprudential, and social arrangement that can be arrived at with moral and logical consistency is a natural order based on private law and radical capitalism with competing, overlapping jurisdictions. A just arrangement of titles to private property is one in which the owners of those titles are free to determine their jurisdiction of private law; it is morally upheld a priori in argumentative discourse that it is the natural right of the private property owner to be able to choose what jurisdiction of private law he seeks to associate with. Private law jurisdictions then will refer to a philosophic body of liberty that synthesizes transcendent apriori libertarian deduction with historical and social knowledge to arrive at a judgement of justice. This is absolutely incremental; limitations on power under radical liberty are not from a formula of check and balances, but from praxeological arguments, the resolution of performative contradictions and their constitution in the form of private law systems. Take the case of the Canon Law of the Catholic Church. The radical liberty of each individual person is assumed as apriori justice derived from the natural law, bound to conscience. The Canon

Law is the Church's human constitution of a mystical body that is received by baptized Christians from the Lord. This reception was not the product of the Lord drafting a treaty composed of hypothetical people, but persons with conscience and soul, acting as free individuals with purposeful actions towards ends; those ends being the constitution of a church only arrived at through cognitive reflection. The mystical body of the church and its laws are synthetic a priori, and cognitive argument allows for the construction of a deontological body of law to be deduced. Because this construction is universal, all private law institutions would be constructed through this method; the church is merely a concrete historical example of this epistemological-praxeological construction The concept of "natural jurisprudence of freedom", fine-tuned by Frank van Dun, is cognitive argumentation as basis of administration of justice. Because the deontological body of right libertarianism are arrived at cognitively through human actors, and because human cognition and action are dimensional, Private law then contains multiple aspects: absolute private law and social private law, in which a unified system of rights binds various jurisdictions that have contracted various households and associations with their own internal codes voluntarily agreed to. Ignoring of then leads to a contradiction in which the non-aggression principle is no longer synthetic a priori knowledge of justice deduced from the natural law and appeal to through conscientious argument, but instead an artificial treaty constructed within a false ecology of human variables, implying an entity presiding over a legal monopoly enforcing the "non-aggression principle. With the corpus of libertarian law and is execution of justice reasoned, a vision of the composition of a libertarian natural order based on private law can be illustrated. Since the appropriation and holding of all titles of property are privatized with the justified proprietor, the emergent private law jurisdictions that would emerge from the free exchanges and relations of the various property owners will be the proprietors defense and justice production (that is, fire, police, arbitration, punishment, policing, and military services.). Jurisdictions will construct a vast network of inter-contractual relations and conduct that are underpinned by the body of universal and unified absolute private law.

Voluntary association will provide a diverse market of jurisdictions possessing distinct vertical orders and cohesion of internal code. You can have the expansion, retreat, or disappearance of some jurisdictions, while you can have the emergence of new jurisdictions that provide superior libertarian governance (strict protection of private property). Because this framework refers to property relations and ethics derives from argumentation, it is an order conceived through conscience involving real people rather than hypothetical actors arranged on the basis of a formula of relations. Karl Ludwig von Haller, a Swiss jurist and early precursor to the anarcho-capitalist libertarianism being argued for, a does an excellent job at conceiving of private law in social and extra-social form and describes a free market of mutual benefit between a vertical order of superiors and inferiors, and contractual obligations binding all of these parties together in trade and production[6]. As jurisprudence is vastly different

---

[6] "According to Haller, the mutually advantageous—noninjurious—character of the natural, vertical, or hierarchical structure of each and every human society is best exemplified by the institution of a family, which also provides the prototype of a natural state. Each family member: father, mother, and child, is subject to the same universal law and entitled to the same rights belonging to every human person: to be free from aggression by another person. Haller terms this law the "absolute" private law. Their association is voluntary and hence mutually beneficial, although never altogether contractual but, most definitely in the case of all children, plain natural or customary and affected also by an element of love. The equality of father, mother and child in terms of "absolute" private law and the voluntary character of their relationship does not imply that they are also equals in regard of what Haller terms "social" (or more appropriately "relative" or "relational") private law, however, which he considers the second, largely customary, much neglected and underdeveloped branch of private law. Rather, the father (or the mother, in matrilineal societies), as the owner of the common household, enjoys more liberties regarding household matters than the mother and child. He is the head of the household, whereas mother and children are his dependents. No one (at least at the dawn of human civilization) ranks above him. He is the household's [proprietor of jurisdiction], subject and subordinate as such solely to the impersonal, eternal and divinely inspired laws of nature, whereas mother and children are also subject and subordinate to his personal authority…To be sure, even as the sovereign ruler of his household the father cannot justifiably do whatever he pleases. Apart from abstaining from aggression against other family members, he is bound

from the legislative conception of the state, the military structure of
this order would also demand a radical return to limited, just warfare

---

by social private law to honor certain contractual or customary obligations
vis-à-vis mother and child (different as these may be in both cases), and the
neglect of these duties vis-à-vis his dependents would release these from their
service obligations toward him. On the other hand, however, any neglect
of duties on the part of mother or child would entitle the father, more far-
reaching and consequential, to exclude or expel them from his household, thus
asserting his very position as [jurisdiction proprietor]…Whether as the result
of natural developments or the [jurisdiction proprietor's] abuse of power and
the dependents' exercise of the right of resistance, then, this if you will 'original
position' of a natural, vertical social order exemplified by a family is bound
to change and change again over time, continuously bringing about new and
more complex types of dependencies and corresponding liberties, expanding or
restricting the range of a [jurisdiction proprietor's] rule, and rendering erstwhile
[jurisdiction proprietor's] lose and former dependents gain [their own justified
properties]." "[T]he system would allow for systematically increased variability
and flexibility of law. Rather than imposing a uniform set of standards onto
everyone (as under statist conditions), insurance agencies could and would
compete against each other not just via price but in particular also through
product differentiation and development. Insurers could and would differ and
distinguish themselves with respect to the behavioral code imposed on and
expected of their clients, with respect to rules of evidence and procedure, and/
or with respect to the sort and assignment of awards and punishments. There
could and would exist side by side, for instance, Catholic insurers applying
Canon law, Jewish insurers applying Mosaic law, Muslims applying Islamic
law, and Non-believers applying Secular law of one variant or another, all of
them sustained by and vying for a voluntarily paying clientele. Consumers
could and would choose, and sometimes change, the law applied to them and
their property. That is, no one would be forced to live under "foreign" law; and
hence, a prominent source of conflict would be eliminated…a system of insurers
offering competing law codes would promote a tendency toward the unification
of law. The "domestic"—Catholic, Jewish, Roman, Germanic, etc.—law would
apply and be binding only on the persons and properties of the insured, the
insurer, and all others insured by the same insurer under the same law. Canon
law, for instance, would apply only to professed Catholics and deal solely with
intra-Catholic conflict and conflict resolution. Yet it would also be possible for
a Catholic to interact, come into conflict with, and wish to be protected from
the subscribers of other law codes…[f]rom this no difficulty would arise so long
as Catholic and Islamic law reached the same or a similar conclusion regarding
the case and contenders at hand."

that was found before the democratic age. Private law demands of jurisdictions that in the event of defending the rights the jurisdiction or other proprietors, defending jurisdictions must make the classical distinction between combatants and non-combatants, the continued freedom of commerce and application of the principle of proportionality in military operations[7]. Economically and ethically superior methods of defense include the use of professionally trained units voluntarily hired, the use of ultra-precise weaponry that carries out an efficient and quick elimination of the target, and the armament of clientele in order to reduce costs of internal defense and as a logical extension of upholding the ethical axiom of private property. Professional units will not only have adequate economic incentive to properly defend clientele but are also tied to the judgements and conclusions of libertarian private law that the objective justice, the jurisdiction(s) they belong to, and obligations and duties that justice compels them to adhere to. The use of modern warfare tactics is expensive and unethical to such an extent that even the most brutish offender would not be able to muster invasions for too long; there needs to be more criminal activity involved to acquire the means for criminal war-making, such as taxation and compulsory education and conscription. In the situation of an attack, companies, ecclesiastical institutions, manors, and other jurisdictions will inform their associates and each other institution of the impending danger and begin to clearly define affected areas that lie within the jurisdiction's corresponding contractual obligations (strictly defined as jurisdictions where the defending party holds justified association with) under invasion from the transgressor force. The defending bodies will begin to direct their military units into the area where they are advised to eliminate the target efficiently and justly as to minimize expenses for greater economic values for both the jurisdiction and its associates, as well as adhering to the judgements of private law as not to be subject to retaliatory punitive justice from other jurisdictions

---

[7]   Hoppe, Hans-Hermann. The Myth of National Defense: Essays on the Theory and History of Security Production. 2003. Ludwig von Mises Institute, Auburn, AL.

defending their associates and their property. Insurance companies, being the private law systems they are, act as lex universitas; this model of the legal corporation treats a corporation more as an autonomous system with rights to constitute internal law codes, rather than an artificial arrangement of limited-liability. There are various cases of successful military leaders using tactics that not only defeated larger and vastly organized powers, but also one that adheres to the libertarian ethic. Consider the various military leaders of the mountainous Spain, the men responsible for the development of what is known as guerilla (Spanish for "little war"). Men like de Zumalacárregui, Ibáñez Cuevas y de Valonga, Martín Díez, and Cura Merino were all important men of noble and clerical extractions who organized the local populace into guerillas, using the mountainous terrain of Spain to their advantage to wreak havoc against the invading Napoleonic forces. The guerilla military tradition would be kept alive through the Carlist and Anarchist movements in Spain, and would slowly be professionalized through proper guerilla training, strategic theory, and arming/equipment. It is always important to keep in mind that these military arrangements were always voluntary and emerged not by sanction of the state, but by a desire to defend personal liberties and rights. Similar guerilla tactics were also found within Early America. Under the organization of our aristocratic Founding Fathers, the American Patriots and Continental Army organized into militias that would utilize the terrain and unpredictability of their tactics. As the war progressed, a mastery of the guerilla tactics culminated in the independence of the Americans, who were able to sustain themselves as a sturdy enterprise that would be able to survive into the future[8]. A defender would have to take into consid-

---

[8] "To the contrary, insurance agencies would encourage the ownership of weapons among their insured by means of selective price cuts. In addition to the opposition of an armed private citizenry, the aggressor state would run into the resistance of not only one but in all likelihood several insurance and reinsurance agencies. In the case of a successful attack and invasion, these insurers would be faced with massive indemnification payments. Unlike the aggressing state, however, these insurers would be efficient and competitive firms…insurers would have to demonstrate defensive readiness vis-à-vis any possible state aggression

eration, at all times, the multitude of causal and teleological aspects of man when protecting the rights of their associates. Because of epistemic limits, and because of the endless inequality and diversity of man, because of the irrefutable reality of the division of labor, defenders within a private law society will always push for peaceful commerce as an end in policy; peaceful commerce allows for social order and the accumulation of wealth, which are the two primary phenomenon defenders are responsible for within libertarian political deontology. Statecraft, being transgressive against economic law and objective morality, cannot be sustained under conditions of human reality. The creation of war and conflict is the most antithetical of all endeavors to human reality; the taxation and proclamations of authority, the maintenance of arms, production, education, health, infrastructure, and political processes demand a contradiction to law. A state must always adopt a principle that does not exist within reality or can be reflected on, such as equality or nationalism, in order to construct a "game" of sorts; an ecology with artificial rules that destroy the division of labor, morality, and humanity. A state must always predestine manageable teleology to all of its human variables, and a state must always predestine the means in order to arrive at those predestined ends that allows for a perpetuation of state power. A defender of property rights will never even inch towards statecraft;

---

to their clients in the form of intelligence services, the ownership of suitable weapons and materials, and military personnel and training. In other words, the insurers would be effectively equipped and trained for the contingency of a state attack and ready to respond with a two-fold defense strategy. On the one hand, insofar as their operations in free territories are concerned, insurers would be ready to expel, capture, or kill every invader while trying to avoid or minimize all collateral damage. On the other hand, insofar as their operations on state territory are concerned, insurers would be prepared to target the aggressor for retaliation. That is, insurers would be ready to counterattack and kill, whether with long-range precision weapons or assassination commandos, state agents from the top of the government hierarchy of king, president, or prime minister on downward while seeking to avoid or minimize all collateral damage to the property of innocent civilians. They would thereby encourage internal resistance against the aggressor government, promote its delegitimization, and possibly incite the liberation and transformation of the state territory into a free country.

the economic cost, the moral transgression, would be impossible to handle without breaching the logic of human action and opting for the Games of the Prince. Whether one opts for a private jurist institution, an ecclesiastical institution, a voluntary policing institution, or a private defense institution, the endless diversity of options cannot be planned here within this work; it would be a contradiction in logic, reasoning, and prose to be overly technical in the reflection upon human action. What can only be done is to put forth synthetic a priori knowledge that is definitively true regarding human action (that people act individually to achieve desired ends, that private property and self-ownership are morally irrefutable truths) and then provide qualitative ideas deduced from that synthetic a priori knowledge. This is never a prescription of how one is to live one's life; it is an absolute proposition of rights and liberty. With that being said, one can look forward to the wonderful age when the laws of liberty triumphantly restore the reality of human action towards the natural order of the universe; the day will be soon, as the Prince has his limits and cannot continue his transgressions against reality any further.

Verticality, Diversity, and Radical Right: The Ontological Structure of Right Libertarian Reality

In the discipline of ontology, one studies the meaning of reality and things, the facts of existence. Reality is the construction and conception of what is true, composed of humans with substantial natures. Reality is governed by laws, as understood in the philosophic body, which govern humanity; reality is transcendent and is reached through personal human cognition and action. Man, in possession of a nature because he is an actor and thinker in reality, is logically different and diverse; one does not need to observe that they are different from one other person, as personal cognition will reveal that I exist in a diverse and vertical reality in which I am not like the other, I exist in vertical and diverse order because individuality of cognition and action affirms so. Individuals think and act with different ends in mind and different means in different ecologies, and this is a universal phenomenon that cannot be altered with any intervention. This phenomenon, being a natural law of transcendent reality, is right and just, and freedom exists when one adheres to it logically and consistently. The alignment of radical natural order libertarianism with "right", "rightism", or a standing within the phenomenon of right to its extremity is therefore logical. Erik von Kuehnelt-Leddihn in his ontological-etymological study of the "right", and "left" lays out to us that these terms are attached to a meaning and serve a purpose in conveying an idea, concept, or phenomenon. The Right, as known, is defined as what is right for man, that is being of justice, law, and freedom; the Right, then, is libertarian and recognizes the ownership of men over themselves, the freedom to develop a unique personality and a reverence for truthful, just traditions, while simultaneously sifting out tyrannical, unjust errors inherited from the past. The Right means freedom, difference, and supports decentralization of decision-making down to the individual, familial, and local level. The Right means private enterprise and laissez-faire in political, economic, and legal life over statist initiation of force and control. Thus, the spectrum can be understood succinctly as this: The Right Extremity is to be represented by a natural order libertarianism; the most extreme representation of Rightist phenomenon and values of personal freedom and its outgrowths of private property and private enterprise, the recognition of the natural difference and inequalities inherent in each individual, the strict adherence to the principles of law and justice can only be represented by an order that is based on the unflinching respect for the nature of man[9].

---

[9]   I am for the word Rightist. Right is right and left is wrong, you see, and in all languages "right" has a positive meaning and "left" a negative one. In Italian, typically, la sinistra is "the left" and il sinistro is "the mishap" or "the calamity." Japanese describes evil as hidar-imae, "the thing in front of the left." And in the Bible, it says in Ecclesiastes, which the Hebrews call Koheleth, that "the heart of the wise man beats on his right side and the heart of the fool on his left…[t] he right has to be identified with personal freedom, with the absence of utopian visions whose realization-even if it were possible-would need tremendous collective efforts; it stands for free, organically grown forms of life. And this in turn implies a respect for tradition. The right is truly progressive, whereas there is no real advance in utopianism which almost always demands-as in the Internationale-to "make a clean sweep" of the past, du passe faisons table rase: dyelayem gladkuyu dosku iz proshlago. If we return to point zero, we are again at the bottom of the ladder, we have to start from scratch again… The true rightist is not a man who wants to go back to this or that institution for the sake of a return; he wants first to find out what is eternally true, eternally valid, and then either to restore or reinstall it, regardless of whether it seems obsolete, whether it is ancient, contemporary, or even without precedent, brand new, "ultramodern." Old truths can be rediscovered, entirely new ones found. The Man of the Right does not have a time-bound, but a sovereign mind… The right stands for liberty, a free, unprejudiced form of thinking, a readiness to preserve traditional values (provided they are true values), a balanced view of the nature of man, seeing in him neither beast nor angel, insisting also on the uniqueness of human beings who cannot be transformed into or treated

as mere numbers or ciphers…The rightists are "federalists", "states' righters" since they believe in local rights and privileges, they stand for the principle of subsidiarity. Decisions, in other words, should be made and carried out on the lowest level-by the person, the family, the village, the borough, the city… [t]he Right recognizes, as a matter of fact, the existence of individual human differences and diversities and accepts them as natural, whereas the Left denies the existence of such differences and diversities or tries to explain them away and in any case regards them as something unnatural that must be rectified to establish a natural state of human equality. The Right recognizes the existence of individual human differences not just with regard to the physical location and make-up of the human environment and of the individual human body… More importantly, the Right also recognizes the existence of differences in the mental make-up of people, i.e., in their cognitive abilities, talents, psychological dispositions, and motivations. It recognizes the existence of bright and dull, smart, and dumb, short-and farsighted, busy, and lazy, aggressive and peaceful, docile and inventive, impulsive and patient, scrupulous and careless people, etc., etc. The Right recognizes that these mental differences, resulting from the interaction of the physical environment and the physical human body, are the results of both environmental and physiological and biological factors. The Right further recognizes that people are tied together (or separated) both physically in geographical space and emotionally by blood (biological commonalities and relationships), by language and religion, as well as by customs and traditions. Moreover, the Right…realizes also that the outcome of input-differences will again be different and result in people with much or little property, in rich and poor, and in people of high or low social status, rank, influence or authority. And it accepts these different outcomes of different inputs as normal and natural…[i]s Libertarianism compatible with the views of the Right or the Left? As for the Right, the answer is an emphatic 'yes.' Every libertarian only vaguely familiar with social reality will have no difficulty acknowledging the fundamental truth of the Rightist worldview. He…indeed must agree with the Right's empirical claim regarding the fundamental not only physical but also mental inequality of man; and he can in particular also agree with the Right's normative claim of "laissez faire," i.e., that this natural human inequality will inevitably result also in unequal outcomes and that nothing can or should be done about this…"; see also Murray Rothbard describe the libertarian's natural position on the extreme right in "Life in the Old Right" and the "Life and Death in the Old Right": "What we have to realize, and we almost have to shake ourselves to believe", writes Rothbard, "is that hard-core libertarians were not considered kooks and crazies; we were treated only as extreme variants of a creed that almost everyone on the Old Right believed: peace, individual liberty, free markets, private property, even the gold standard. And since we were simply consistent upholders of a creed which the entire Old Right believed, we were

17

In contrast, the greatest enemy of liberty, which being equality, is merely anti-human tyranny and destruction that is irrespective of basic ontological structure of reality; equality is a praxeological impossibility, a dreamed up end that, regardless of how much collectivization commences, will never come into existence. Libertarianism is diametrically opposed to the notion of equality as unnatural, as equality must be enforced through the initiation of force, the violation of absolute private property rights, and violent abolition of the division of labor and social hierarchies in totality. The egalitarian ethic is antagonistic and antithetical to liberty also on the grounds of its objections to individuality and preference; the individual person must be chastised and forbidden to be superior, to be industrious,

---

able, though small in number, to influence and permeate the views of the broad mass of Old Right Americans. It was a happy symbiosis." Rothbard confirms my political scientific thesis of libertarianism (Or as Kuehnelt-Leddihn spoke of, true liberalism) being the philosophical worldview of the entire Right, with the anarcho-capitalist tradition representing the most pure and extreme form of liberty and private enterprise. As well, traditionalism (Or genuine decentralist conservatism identified by Hoppe as libertarian) has an incredibly important role within a natural order of liberty, as a defense of the natural order must be a conscious social effort. In "A New Fusionism," Rothbard expounds the natural affinities of real libertarianism and genuine traditionalism (conservatism): "For, as became evident at the JRC meeting and has been clear for some time, this new movement is far more than an "alliance," which implies two inherently separate entities. Paleolibertarianism and paleoconservatism is increasingly a great coming together, a fusion of different but complementary elements." Rothbard goes on to describe the real manifestation of such affinities: "The point of the panels was not to score debating points but to try to find common ground, and "convergence" was achieved with remarkable ease on almost every point. The only protesters were those few libertarians and traditionalists in the audience who suffered from culture shock, facing this ongoing paleo-dialogue for the first time. By the end of the day, however, even some of them showed signs of adjusting to the new dispensation" For as I, Hoppe, Rothbard, and Kuehnelt-Leddihn have observed, libertarianism is an extreme variant of the rightist principles of liberty, property, diversity, private enterprise, law and justice against leftist vices of statism, slavery, equality, uniformity, war, and tyranny. Traditionalism also provides the second prong attack that compliments libertarian political-economic-legal analysis to form a grand defense and exposition of a Right society.

intelligent, or virtuous. It is scandalous for man to stratify, as this renders him unpredictable, nonconforming and unformulaic, difficult to impossible to control. Man must be at an even level with his fellow man; man must look horizontally shoulder-to-shoulder, and never in a vertical head-to-toe fashion, view each other as individual grains of sand in a massive heap of sand. A return to absolute private property rights will lead to a vast increase in variety, diversity, hierarchies(verticality) and just discrimination. Because exclusivity is the logical implication of private property, there will be vast differences in association and standards of entry. Attempts to disturb this natural difference in the division of labor is bound to be a disaster, damning men back into collectivist primitivism and degeneracy. Inequality is essential to the emergence of a division of labor, as under a division of labor, individuals specialize in their unequal, different professions, and lines of production. Industry, superiority, and nobility are welcomed as civilization and right (free, lawful, and just) developments within social order. Attempts to erase inequality lead to the absence of exchange and production; as the Day-Two Problem demonstrates that any exchange, whether saving, investment, or consumption, will lead to unequal, different outcomes and thus requires corrective force to undo market exchange; superior individuals will manage larger estates and capital than inferior individuals, and forceful redistribution of titles from superior/just hands into inferior/unjust hands is bound to go left into a disaster. In following logic, two postulates can be concluded about egalitarianism. One, production and exchange are forbidden by egalitarianism, as unequal, diverse, and vertical realities of human talents and action are the very nature of production and exchange. The egalitarian stipulates that one must do everything; regardless of if, factually, he cannot. Two, this means that the egalitarian opposes human nature and the structure and manifestation of reality itself. The egalitarian, ipso facto, has a paranoid obsession with collectivizing private life and maintaining a gigantic state apparatus that has totalitarian control over the past, present, and future and agitates for the swift abolition of all three under the guillotine in favor of an antiexistence[10]. No real growth is allowed; for growth, to the egalitarian, is the ultimate sin. The Left Extremity is, then, to be represented by Total State and Total Collectivization: the extreme representation of egalitarian uniformity can be found within Communism; as stated before, no one is to pursue his different preferences and paths with his own property and self-steering, and they are to act in strict horizontality[11]. For Left means being of a sinister

---

[10] "Furthermore, Marx was completely ignorant of the fact that each participant in the division of labor cooperates through the market economy, exchanging for each other's products and increasing the productivity and living standards of everyone. To Marx, any differences between men and, therefore, any specialization in the division of labor, is a "contradiction," and the communist goal is to replace that "contradiction" with harmony among all. This means that to the Marxist any individual differences, any diversity among men, are "contradictions" to be stamped out and replaced by the uniformity of the antheap. Friedrich Engels maintained that the emergence of the division of labor shattered the alleged classless harmony and uniformity of primitive society and was responsible for the cleavage of society into separate and conflicting classes. Hence, for Marx and Engels, the division of labor must be eradicated in order to abolish class conflict and to usher in the ideal harmony of the "classless society," the society of total uniformity."

[11] "[B]ut the left is the advocate of the opposite principles. It is the enemy of diversity and the fanatical promoter of identity. Uniformity is stressed in all leftist utopias, a paradise in which everybody should be the "same," where envy is dead, where the "enemy" either no longer exists, lives outside the gates, or is utterly humiliated. Leftism loathes differences, deviation, stratifications. Any hierarchy it accepts is only "functional." The term "one" is the keynote: There should be only one language, one race, one class, one ideology, one religion, one type of school, one law for everybody, one flag, one coat of arms and one centralized world state…[t]he Left on the other hand is convinced of the fundamental equality of man, that all men are "created equal." It does not deny the patently obvious, of course: that there are environmental and physiological differences, i.e., that some people live in the mountains and others on the seaside, or that some men are tall and others short, some white and others black, some male and others female, etc. But the Left does deny the existence of mental differences or, insofar as these are too apparent to be entirely denied, it tries to explain them away as "accidental." That is, the Left either explains such differences as solely environmentally determined, such that a change in environmental circumstances would produce an equal outcome, and it denies that these differences are caused (also) by some—comparatively

nature, uniformity, ugliness, slavery, tyranny. Communism, National Socialism, Fascism, Social Democracy, and Progressivism are all ideologies of the Left, for their ideological support for the state and collective control and the creation, not discovery and interpretation, of law. All reject personal freedom in favor of utopian equality and are materialistic instead of moralistic. The policy and governance of the Left is antilibertarian and procrustean; the individual person cannot become too elite, but also cannot become a worthless mouth breather who is a burden on the collective. There must always be a permanent initiation of force in order to maintain equality. It is no mistake that Mao Tse-Tsung, Joseph Stalin, Adolf Hitler, Benito Mussolini, and all other modern totalitarians wore military uniforms; compared to distinguished aristocratic clothing or glamorous industrial capitalists, they were the personification of the uniform, horizontal general will rather than the personalistic-individualistic themes of aristocratic tastes. These dictators, after all, were men of the People, the fraternity of the nation rather than the patriarchy of the free and just fatherland or country. While Tse-Tsung, Stalin, and Hitler belong to the school of the Radical Socialist Total State, our other ideologies of the Left belong to the school of the Social Democratic Total State. While the Radical Socialists want Total Collectivism, the Social Democrats are more akin to appealing to gradualism and compromise; do not take down the capitalist in a socialist revolution, but slowly begin to socialize his purpose for socialist ends. The social democrat intends on intervening in the delicate process of planning that a capitalist undertakes for his capital, or an aristocrats influence over a community; through democracy, 'we' can 'hold accountable' a supposed

---

intractable—biological factors. Or else, in those cases where it cannot be denied that biological factors play a causal role in determining success or failure in life…the Left considers these differences as pure luck and the resulting outcome of individual success or failure as undeserved. In any case, whether caused by advantageous or disadvantageous environmental circumstances or biological attributes, all observable individual human differences are to be equalized…[T]he Left insists that the undeservedly "lucky" must compensate the "unlucky" so that every person will be accorded an "equal station in life," in correspondence with the natural equality of all men."

hoarding on the behalf of superiors to 'share' with the greater collective their productive enterprises and social influence. The social democrat over time envisions the egalitarian socialist state being the product of a "learned" democratic "benevolence" by the superiors of society, not needing to shed a drop of blood or fire a single bullet.

High Catholicity as the Metaphysical Theological Existence of Man.

A category of faith exists within all men; there are ends in which the criticism of reason cannot explain. Given such, those categories of mind and action within the natural order that deal with the composition of teleology are metaphysical. Metaphysical teleology deals with theological existence; how one serves, how one manners, how one fulfills the Lord his end. The metaphysics of theological existence is not detached from reality; it is concerned with what is above, and it attached to human reality by the fact that reality is composed of human actors with teleological ends. Theological existence is where the cultural qualities of man, his literature, aesthetics, and tastes descends downward from. Of course, the Catholic Church is the mother institution that bears and presides over the theological existence of man; she is the rock inaugurated through the Lord to bring home the children of his Father back into his Kingdom. It is through Christ and towards Christ that we are to lead an existence that is holy and within his image; our existence must emulate him in his creativity, generosity, and individual independence. The carnal chimera of the status quo will always bear hostility to our higher human person; mediocrity exists by restricting those who stratify. Shunned we of Christ are for violating a divinized ecology with our industry, arrogant and cranky we our for originality in intellect, backwards we are for our responsibilities to family and kin. Mediocrity inquires to the Christian, "why create when you can be content with the state of the world and the Prince who presides over it?" The

Christian, with strength and independence, opts to turn the cheek to the trickery of the Prince. He is aware of what the Prince demands from him; that is, he replace the Lord with himself, that he accepts the status quo, that he prestige the states of the world and its mediocre amalgamations of all unethical and uncreative tragedies. Instead of laughing at the chimera of the Prince's mediocrity, instead of ridiculing him for his egalitarian envy of Christ's position as the Son of God, the Prince demands your flesh, your submission to his management by reduction away from God's beloved creation into his number, his statistic. The Prince will tempt you always with his psycho-trickery, his mob, his state. He seeks to explain away your individuality and creative work with the various labels and shackles of pathology, of diagnosis with "deviation". With a nasty venom coaxed under superficiality, the Prince twists the Christ to serve his end of power; he oft pontificate that all he does is within charity, usually with unreflective verbosity and number magic to mask the hollow reality. When one resists, he seeks to control you with the withdrawal of things material and flesh; the Prince desires your starvation, hoping your spirit will collapse inward towards him and away from He who he envies. The Christian knows that he must build and create, in emulation of his spiritual Father in Heaven, to allow God the Holy Spirit to course and embrace his temple and body. This phenomenon is reflected in the Christian concepts of duty, "have a son, plant a tree, write a book." In my own rendition, I expand this to include "to make a product, to provide a good or service," which is related to "plant a tree." The Christian, in his theological existence, pursues creative ends in all capacities within the division of labor with the talents he possesses; if he wastes his talents, or concedes them to the Prince's number, he is not leading a life after and toward the Lord. First, to have a son, to plant a tree, to write a book means more than the merely birthing of a male offspring, or the management of an arboretum, or the scribing of a chronicle; it means to educate a young boy out of infancy, into masculine fatherhood; to build or produce something that produces, that creates value, and to bring to the tongue those things of the intellect and imagination. Central to one's theological existence is the nuclear family established after the patterns of a primary father, his wife, and the offspring that they bear together. Within the home the Christian concept of agape is fostered by the cultivation of catholicity a father and mother are responsible for; to guide their children both through the world, away from the Prince, and towards our Three Person'd God in heaven. Only the Lord can appoint to you your True Father; biology is only half of the determinant. The parents have a love-based obligation for their children to succeed and realize their objective and real excellence; as for all of human history, the success of children means the success of humanity and the fulfillment of theological existence. Education, with a Latin etymology meaning "growth", is always attached to the home and to the parents; growth needs a well-grounded home in order to successfully come into fruition. Because of agape, of ultimate charity and love, does there exist a trust in the children to take on the risks of a patehmata mathemata; growth marked by rigor, intensity, erudition, adventure, near-trauma, and scholastic method and reasoning that calls upon the faculties of originality and personality that can come from within. The cultivation of intellect then, with scholastic instruction and self-driven learning as its two major components, can only be done by private education solutions and ultimately the parents of the child. Theorists of education are usually mediocre; however, uncommon men such as Murray Rothbard, ahead and creative in his contribution, advocated a natural order of education based within the home against the Prince's laboratory rat box. Rothbard deplores the Prince's takeover of education from 1880-1920, and he correct the historical record to reflect the reality of the Prince's action and goals. Rothbard was fully aware of what the public "schools" were intended to achieve; rather than teaching children critical thinking, language, and history, the public schools instead teach egalitarianism and group-think. Their goal is the severing and destruction of the intellect, and instead, the inculcation of stupidity. The progressivists constructed their nefarious educationist gallows throughout the end of the 19th and early 20th Centuries; the war against the enemies of the egalitarian collectivist utopia was to be a totalitarian one, modeled after the patterns of those nasty and rapacious Jacobin state terrorists[12]. Important insights into how this laboratory-condition system of schooling was to be constructed were made by Murray Rothbard in his "Education: Free and Compulsory." A succinct history of education in the modern world was detailed by Rothbard, beginning with Martin Luther's conflicts with the Catholic Church, John Calvin's political and religious legacy all the way up to 19th Century Prussia and American Progressivism. Under the absolutist rule of Frederick Wilhelm III, the Prussians inaugurated the tyrannical Civil Service that was to keep afloat the militaristic order of the state. After embarrassing loses to Napoleon's France in Alsace-Lorraine, the Prussian Civil Service was quick to put the blame upon the individual; he is too individualistic, his allegiances too close to the papacy, too apathetic to contribute to the great Prussian experiment of militaristic German rule. Private education and scholasticism had to be done away with; a good soldier, a good servant does not critically think or analyze, but rather, is coercible, moldable. Parental dominion over the education and development of their children, the influence of religion in general and the Catholic Church in particular, had to swiftly and effectively be eliminated so the powerful Civil Service can "raise" children to serve. American educationists flocked over to the education colleges and psychology labs of central Europe to admire and replicate the mechanisms of control and leveling offered by these state servants; from Horace Mann to G. Stanley Hall and his students, the new methods of standardization, the use of rote word-picture instruction in reading, and the emphasis on collective work dazzled the Prince's educationist number desk-workers seeking to install social engineering apparatuses in the United States. As noted by Rothbard again in the Progressive Era, the Yankee Postmillenarian Pietists sought out to stampede The great design of the state "schooling" system was the intentional pathologizing of children into isolated,

---

[12] "The eminent University of Wisconsin sociologist Edward Alsworth Ross, a favorite of Theodore Roosevelt and the veritable epitome of a progressive social scientist, summed it up thus: The role of the public official, and in particular of the public school teacher, is "to collect little plastic lumps of human dough from private households and shape them on the social kneading board."

broken, unfree pieces[13]. These agents of the state were fully abreast as to what composed the great Western tradition; personal individualism, scholastic learning in complement to independent learning, and diversity were the hallmarks of social discourse and order that had to be done away with. The first stages of overcoming these natural limitations against power came first through systematic expropriation of resources to erect the accrediting system of number. With the accrediting system in place, its educationist guillotines of mass democracy, standardized testing and positive-negative reinforcement sched-

---

[13] "Children indifferent to the adult world of values and accomplishment, defying the universal human experience laid down over thousands of years that a close study of grown-ups is always the most exciting and one of the most necessary occupations of youth. Have you noticed how very few people, adults included, want to grow up anymore? Toys are the lingua franca of American society for the masses and the classes. Children with almost no curiosity. Children who can't even concentrate for long on things they themselves choose to do. Children taught to channel-change by a pedagogy employing the strategy "and now for something different," but kids who also realize dimly that the same damn show is on every channel. Children with a poor sense of the future, of how tomorrow is linked to today. Children who live in a continuous present. Conversely, children with no sense of the past and of how the past has shaped and limited the present, shaped and limited their own choices, predetermined their values and destinies to an overwhelming degree. Children who lack compassion for misfortune, who laugh at weakness, who betray their friends and families, who show contempt for people whose need for help shows too plainly. Children condemned to be alone, to age with bitterness, to die in fear. Children who can't stand intimacy or frankness. Children who masquerade behind personalities hastily fabricated from watching television and from other distorted gauges of human nature. Behind the masks lurk crippled souls. Aware of this, they avoid the close scrutiny intimate relationships demand because it will expose their shallowness of which they have some awareness. Materialistic children who assign a price to everything and who avoid spending too much time with people who promise no immediate payback—a group which often includes their own parents. Children who follow the lead of schoolteachers, grading and ranking everything…Everything simplified into simple-minded categories by the implied judgment of a cash price, deemed an infallible guide to value. Dependent children who grow up to be whining, treacherous, terrified, dependent adults, passive and timid in the face of new challenges. And yet this crippling condition is often hidden under a patina of bravado, anger, aggressiveness."

ules("grading"), from the kindergartens all the way up to post-graduate study, enabled the creation of any public effect they wish; in our current situation, that public effect is a mass without any individuality, originality, erudition; a mass that is dependent and infantile, a mass that doesn't question their deficiencies due to their inability to think critically or receive criticism, a mass that was handsomely rewarded through the evasion of the guillotine for rewards of material and libertine scores and approval. The educationist is only concerned with the perpetual maintenance of a corporate fascist collective that relies on the lack of independence and intellect of its civil servants. The high intellectuals, the shrewd, and the wise have their heads severed under the Prince and his educationists for not conforming to the Iron Bed of Stupidity that the Age of the Fish agitates so vociferously for. The stupefying effects of mass "education" or crowd "education" must be understood; all will learn nothing, and all will be reduced to the level of the weakest link. With the massive apparatus of standardized testing and reinforcement schedules, one can indeed arbitrarily install the aforementioned obedience, dependency, and rote learning as the standard that should be achieved, and one can preemptively manipulate the type of "intellectual" discourse and "productivity" that takes place within the system. This is achieved through removing responsibility of and outright punishing and discouraging justificatory argument, rigorous analytical consistency, and creativity through the reduction of the faculties to number, mass, dead statistics[14]. The decline in the quality of academic research and

---

[14] Not until much later, when I had seen something of mass-education and observed its results, did I perceive how great this advantage is. With Mark Hopkins on one end of a log and a student on the other, the student gets the best out of Hopkins and gets as much of it as he can absorb; the law of diminishing returns does not touch him. Add twenty students, and neither he nor the twenty gets the same thing; add two hundred, and it is luck if anybody gets anything remotely like the same thing..."[I]n England the public school which fostered the herd instinct. To be different was treason and indecency. The religious principles of old were replaced by taboos. The return to primitive society had begun. The British public school with its latent suspicion for brilliancy and originality is largely responsible for the depersonalization of the English upper class. (The Scottish mountain dwellers fared definitely better.)

The public school had fostered a team spirit and a small herd esprit de corps which is neither aristocratic nor of great value…by its tendency to create reliable mediocrities. One is inclined to like the gentleman of a Byronic pattern rather than the one standardized by the old school tie, and to prefer an aristocracy…to one crushed in the years of adolescence by a vaguely homoerotic group spirit… Boarding schools, preparatory schools, and public schools are far more hostile to the ideals of liberty than the much maligned family, and this is the reason why these actually play into the hands of democratism…The ochlocratic state on the other side needs human sheep who become party members. We must bear in mind that a two-party system in which the parties are not divided by philosophical differences is the only meager guarantee of a survival of political democracy** The plurality of philosophical antagonistic parties dug the grave of political democracy in Germany, France, Austria, Spain, and Italy. In order to save and preserve the uniformity of the political philosophy which not only dominates the intellectual scene of a country but also constitutes the common denominator of the two parties, strong social and educational sanctions are necessary; only an open or silent agreement between all the opinion-forming agencies (press, radio, school, cinema, publishing, advertising) can keep this rigid uniformity. The full cooperation of society, which possesses after all the most potent sanctions, is an indispensable pre-requisite. Education, in the new totalitarian democracies, must also have necessarily a low standard in order to prevent a development of the critical faculties of the individual…different use of this theory; they enlarged humanity by including the animals and Darwin's assertion that the brain of an ant is the most wonderful particle of the world, more wonderful perhaps than the human brain, is characteristic for the trend of the time. The ants had their eulogy written in the early twentieth century by Maurice Maeterlinck, and Waldemar Bonsels delighted in sentimental tales about the life of the bees. But great savants like Father Wasmann, S.J., exploded the myth of the "intelligence" of these extremely uniformistic insects who live in strict, unvarying discipline…[t]hings which are "measurable" are popular [in a statist order based on mass collectivism] because they can be "judged" by the masses who are thankful for the criterion of numbers. The circenses of today are based on "scorings." One could, if one wanted to, compare universities by taking their scorings at spelling bees or football teams as a basis for comparison. Authors may thus be compared by their literary output, the number of pages they have written or the reprintings of their books. But could one arrange a "match" between two savants? Hardly! It certainly would be amusing to see a race for holiness between two prospective saints. And painters? Pictures may be measured by square inches and even poems by yards. All this cannot be proposed in earnest and the fact remains that spiritual and intellectual values cannot be measured as quantities. They cannot be expressed in numerals as, for instance, the sex appeal of the film stars, which is frequently evaluated by

intellectuals can be attributed to this; the phenomenon of hyper-specialization, scientism, cultural rot, artistic ugliness, penny press language, short-sighted planning, lack of analytical rigor, mass democracy, and pervasive relativism and positivism are all products of an anti-intellectual arrangement based upon quantities and scores found within worthless games that work preposterously under the façade of "achievement" and "evaluation". Public "education" necessitates the rejection of scholastic learning. The public "education" system does not see, nor can it see, individuals with unique backgrounds and origin, but rather, pieces from the same mass to be molded into utopian cogs. With its impersonal and standardized ways, intelligence is punished as there is absolutely no introspection involved in the evaluation and assessment of students. The status quo of "education", then, really amounts to antieducation; one enters these institutions

---

its financial effect on the box office…For anyone who is capable of learning, his or her knowledge and actions cannot logically be regarded as determined by a complex of causes operating in a constant way (whether statistically or deterministically). There can only be constants in relation to the causes of events where one is dealing with a world of nonlearning objects, or more correctly, where one conceives of an objective sphere of reality as a world of nonlearning objects. One cannot, however, think of one-self as nonlearning. Not only is an intellect functioning in accordance with the constancy principle necessarily a learning intellect (we learn about how objects conceived of as nonlearning behave), but the statement "I can learn" also proves to hold true in other respects. It is in principle not falsifiable, for in order to falsify it one would need to be able to learn. And from another point of view, one cannot justifiably argue against the statement since, qua argument, there must be possible replies to it, and as the validity of an argument (as opposed to that of a stimulus) would be independent of the nature of the reply, such possible replies must be regarded as contingent reactions, and therefore it must be possible to learn. No scientific advance can ever alter the fact that one must regard one's knowledge and actions as uncaused. One might hold this conception of "freedom" to be an illusion, and from the point of view of a "scientist" with cognitive powers substantially superior to any human, that is, from the point of view of God, such a description may well be correct. However, we are not God, and even if freedom is illusory from His standpoint, for us human beings it is a necessary illusion. We cannot predict in advance the future states of our knowledge and the actions manifesting that knowledge on the basis of previous states; we can only reconstruct them after the event

with an intellectual development higher than they leave them. With a secure natural order of education restored, the maturation of the individual can successfully commence, and the important hereditary duties of property and family are once again acknowledged and practiced. What is a homeschooling/private education curriculum to look like, however? I can fashion what scholasticity would entail; serious study that is interdisciplinary in scope in which a student is to study and meditate upon written and oral literature found within the literary canon, demonstrations of competency and then demonstrate mastery through infrequent but through and reflective oral examination, one that is thorough and interested in the initiation of discourse. A master of a work is one who familiarizes themselves with prior knowledge, provides original contribution and creative insight, and conduct sound instruction to those seeking to acquire greater knowledge and arrive at the truth. In contrast to accrediting schedules, scholasticity is derived from justificatory argument for objective reality and truth; scholasticity is based on the study of real people, of real relations and truths, rather than artificial people with arbitrary standards that have no root in reality. This curriculum is based on the concept of the personality; one is free to pursue their competencies to the fullest extent without having to be subject to the injustices of forced rudiment or predestinarian molds, stripped of intelligent order and erudition. For under scholasticity the endless inequality, verticality, and diversity is accepted as apriori fact of human action and recognizes that an equal mold is anathema to reality. With that being said, it is one's duty now to propose a constructive model of what a natural order of education is to look like; what curriculum most conducive to the emergence of radical liberty and high tradition. St. John Henry Newman, the great Catholic cardinal and intellectual, promotes a liberal arts curriculum that is centered around the cultivation of culture, the systematic and interdisciplinary presentation of knowledge so as to allow for complete and consistent understanding and improved faculties of critical thinking and philosophical reflection. Newman understood the importance of moral principle as the foundation end of liberal education as compared to aimless rote characteristic of inculcating statist variables. You are not to please an intellectually limited "grader" whose praise, quite frankly, is utterly worthless; one pursues philosophy out of a deontological devotion to the high intellect, out of personal responsibility, out of charity and love. You are to bind your conscience to the truth with the creation of original and systematic work, at any pace that allows for consistent and diligent cultivation. It was well known to philosophers of all doctrines that education and thinking is the opposite of a game; games are anathema to contemplation. The achievements that one is to present is their own original work, whose value exists within the work itself to then be received in critical discourse as opposed to aligning work against a predestined mold that in limited in epistemic scope. As an extension of the lesson at hand, theological existence means that one must always derive their self from within, never from any external force. All forces of the status quo, as has been emphasized, are under the tutelage of the Prince; it is he who demands your slavery and your soul for tribute to the pulsating chimera of the carnal. The Prince desires the ungrounded, the

The History of Man and the Zeitgeist of the Status Quo

Libertarian analysis of historical events, especially anarcho-capitalist strands, has been faced with the task of reinvestigating mainstream interpretations of historical events. The libertarian, through the pure deductive theory of its moral philosophy, concludes the State is born out of warfare and destruction; not production and exchange, and the State is the source of perpetual conflict and social decline. This requires the libertarian, then, to subject to scrutiny the current presentation of the state as a positive and just development in the fostering of peaceful and civilized human affairs. For the best, most logical-libertarian answer, begin first by consulting Hans-Hermann Hoppe, who charts a grand historical narrative that deals with the decline of social order, beginning with the stateless, aristocratic, natural order of competing jurisdictions that marked the European Middle Ages. "What I mean by natural aristocrats, nobles and kings here," Hoppe writes, "is simply this: In every society of some minimum degree of complexity, a few individuals acquire the status of a natural elite. Due to superior achievements of wealth, wisdom, bravery, or a combination thereof, some individuals come to possess more authority than others and their opinion and judgment commands widespread respect." The decline of the natural aristocracy can be pinpointed to the philosophy of Machiavellianism, which promoted the use of aggressive means to consolidate power to a single "princedom" that would be the sovereign over the political economy of a given territory. The lessons from the prince made its way across the European continent to the kings of the realms; absolute monarchy arose in the seventeenth century as a revolt against the natural aristocracy and independence of the ecclesiastical hierarchy through an appeal to the masses, promoting egalitarian propaganda that would undermine the voluntarily acquired authority of these jurisdictions. It mixed these egalitarian ideologies still with monarchical rule; this monarch was completely unrestricted by precedent or private institutions, as he had corporatized them into his court through Machiavellian means. This developing sovereign state was officially imposed with the regrettable Treaty of Westphalia, a watershed development abolishing anything resembling overlapping jurisdiction. The kings were able to establish within their sovereign territories which church was allowed to teach and exert authority, a decision made in absence of deducing from the jurisprudence of the natural law. Now that sovereign states were artificially imposed over the stateless natural order in Europe, the king now held a territorial monopoly of violence from an imperial seat over a given territory. The democratic rhetoric utilized by the monarchs against the aristocrats would turn out to contain the seeds to this regime's own destruction, however, and the ideas of democracy and constitutional monarchy would see a massive emergence with the French Revolution[15].

Democratic forms of government began to justify their rule through the declaration that the people contained within the sovereign states had collective ownership of the state, and that all men

---

[15] It should be noted that democratic movements had been spawned with the Protestant Reformation and the Czech Hussites, as well as the Taborites many centuries before. The French Revolution was merely an explosion of collectivist ideology that had brewed with the Hussites proto-National Socialism, the ensuing Protestant Reformation that even its former protagonist, Martin Luther, admits was a "Pandora's Box" that allowed for the proliferation of "craziness and frenzy of the masses." As Hans-Hermann Hoppe pointed out, Absolute Monarchy was a left-wing deviation from traditional monarchy to the middle-of-the-road corporate state, for the absolutists employed egalitarian programs in order to centralize control away from the thousands of aristocrats across the European continent to themselves, proclaiming to represent "the people." The egalitarian ideologies also served as the basis for democratic-republican government that would then overtake absolute monarchy and lead to a further drift from libertarianism; the state was now publicly controlled within a horizontal order of numerical mediocrity.

were entitled to have the ability to rule and manage the state. From here, Hans-Hermann Hoppe points out that the French Revolution's reintroduction of democracy was a declining, decivilizing factor that led to the emergence of totalitarianism across the globe; Soviet communism, German national socialism, Italian fascism, American social democracy, and internationalist corporatism that would compound short-sighted, unlawful and economically destructive governance. This ushering in of democracy would culminate in World War I and World War II, with their notable redefining of wars as totalitarian and large-scale. Wars had previously been very small-scale and defined, but now entire nations went to war with each other in the interest of establishing ideological supremacy and control over new populations and territories. All resources, material, and human, were now to be mobilized for the war effort at the expense of private production and interests. Erik von Kuehnelt-Leddihn, in his Monarchy and War, as well as his other works, observes the identitarian characteristics of democratic equality as a primary catalyst for this new development in warfare. Beginning first with the French Jacobins as a precursor to National Socialism, then finally arriving at Hitler and the NSDAP, he observes that a collective hatred has been supplanted within the masses, demonizing the enemy to be portrayed as a different other that must be levelled. This serves as the state's justification for mass-murder and barbaric acts of war, for seizure of private property and the withering of personal freedoms. The masses are then desensitized to indiscriminate killing; why must I show the different other any form of mercy or respect, for they have done me trouble by being unlike me? The different other is an alien oppressor who is trying to ravage my group through whatever means that can utilize, whether that be capitalist and aristocratic institutions or churches and religious orders, so it would be even desirable to gore the enemy in the cruelest of ways! Karl Marx and Friedrich Engels were known for holding Anti-Slavic bigotry, viewing Slavs as primitives and supporting Prussian Imperialism Eastward into Serbia, Poland, and Russia as a modernizing force against this Slavic recusancy and nonconformity[16]. Soviet Communism took identitarianism further and began to create an "Us Versus Them" dichotomy between the Party and the anti-Party, the conforming and nonconforming. The people opposed to the Communist Party line and agenda were "bourgeois agents" and thus needed to be physically crushed and defeated, deported, or utterly humiliated; to be without property, without platforms for intellectual exchange, without means to travel. The Soviets succeeded in doing this to the Ukrainian Anarchists in the 1920's, and throughout the communist regime with property owners, businessmen, priests, foreigners, and citizenry rebelling against their new totalitarian slavery. Mao Tse-Tung's Cultural Revolution was among humanity's most atrocious episodes, in rounding up landlords and landlord sympathizers to be humiliated and executed, in which it is believed that deaths could have soared to 300 to 400 million deaths total during Chinese Communist rule alone[17] (Not

---

[16] For more on Socialist Racism, see Marx, Karl; The Russian Menace; "This splendid territory [the Balkans] has the misfortune to be inhabited by a conglomerate of different races and nationalities, of which it is hard to say which is the least fit for progress and civilization. Slavonians, Greeks, Wallachians, Arnauts, twelve millions of men, are all held in submission by one million of Turks, and up to a recent period, it appeared doubtful whether, of all these different races, the Turks were not the most competent to hold the supremacy which, in such a mixed population, could not but accrue to one of these nationalities.

[17] "The havoc wrought by leftism is simply colossal. If humanity had any common sense, had been permanently endowed with reason, knowledge, a sense of history, it would have renounced the leftist gods a long time ago. The left, however, has by far the better catchwords, and man's brain power has to be viewed in terms of potentiality, not of actuality. It needs enormous moral and spiritual qualities to mobilize one's intelligence fully; it just does not work automatically. However, an unbiased glance backward and around us reveals an ocean of misery, unmitigated horror, and colossal stupidity: the fiendish massacres perpetrated by the French Revolution, the noyades, the batteries nationales, the blood orgies in the Vendee, the forests of guillotines, the silly and vain risings of 1848, the bestialities of the Paris Commune, with its mass slayings of innocent hostages, the senseless overthrow of the Mexican and Brazilian monarchies which alone could have insured an orderly development to these two big Latin American nations. There is the suicidal order of 1919 in Central Europe which provoked World War II, the idiotic transformation of Germany into a republic,

the ignominious treatment of Hungary and Bulgaria that forced them into the Axis camp; the horrors of the Russian Revolution and the hell of Stalinism culminating in Katyn and the icy inferno of the kontslageri on two Continents; the Nazi Revolution with its countless bestialities, the "Kazetts" and the extermination camps; the "democratic" aerial warfare that burned alive myriads of noncombatants of all ages, the infamous cruelties of the Spanish Loyalists and the Chinese "agrarian reformers"; the sadistic doings of totalitarian police forces in Poland, Hungary, Czechoslovakia, Rumania, Bulgaria, Yugoslavia, and Albania; the fiendish tortures applied in North Vietnam and North Korea; the un-peaking depredations of the Mexican, Cuban, Colombian, and Venezuelan "Revolutions"; the nightmares of decolonization in India and the Congo, in Angola and Mozambique, in the Cameroons and the Sudan; the brutalities of Genosse Ulbricht's repression of the Berlin Rising, of dear old Khrushchev's quelling of the Hungarian Revolution-not to forget the millions of Kulaks deported, starving and dying; the famines in the Ukraine and in the Kuban Region; the deportation of untold East Germans, Sudeten Germans, East Poles, Latvians, Lithuanians, Estonians, Krim-Tartars, Volga-Germans, and even the Communist victims of Stalin caught in their own net. Remember the French massacred by the Communists working within the Resistance, the Italians assassinated by their own Reds, the Yugoslavs victimized by the Partizani. Remember the slaughter of the Domobranci by Tito (surrendered to him by the British), the fate of the Vlassovtsy (surrendered jointly by the Americans and the British), the scenes of terror at Dachau, when the Nazi cremation stoves were hardly cold, and the Western Allies packed good Russians into railroad cars to have them shipped as traitors to the Soviet Union-desperate men then tried to commit suicide by biting their arteries. Think of the innocent victims of Red Chinese bands in the jungles of Malaya, of Catholics executed in Mexico, of the Lutheran pastors slain in Riga, of the 256 human roasts in the Montagnard Village of Dak-Son, the 4,000-odd Christians slain in Hue, the buried Benedictines of Thien-An. If one were to take paper and pencil to make an estimate of how many people were murdered or killed in battle because of the ideas of the French Revolution in their various stages, guises, and evolutionary forms, because of the ideas of equality, ethnic or racist identity, a "classless society," a "world safe for democracy," a "racially pure people," true social justice achieved by social engineering"—one would arrive at simply staggering sums. Even the Jewish holocaust offered by the National Socialists with five or six million dead would seem almost a drop in the bucket. There must have been at least 120 or 150 Million victims, perhaps even three hundred million. The victims of the French Revolution were relatively few, but sadistic bestiality had entered Western Civilization through that door, and we have had increasingly "bigger and better" slaughters ever since-as the Western World moves nearer and nearer to the abyss." See Kuehnelt-Leddihn, Erik Ritter von. Leftism: From

even including the Great Leap Forward!) The American Homeland has also felt the affront of democratic decivilization in a much less blood-soaked and primitive but rivaling destructionism and tyranny. The United States in particular, since its inception, has taken a twisted, deviant turn towards welfare-warfare statism. While belonging to the same lineage as Communism, welfare-warfare Statism differed in one aspect: it did not advocate total collectivization through the revolutionary means taken elsewhere; it advocated instead for corporate tripartite cooperation between the state, business, and labor. Through three crucial historical developments, social-democratic statism asserts itself as the American style of socialism: The Northern invasion of the South, the Progressive Era in general and the establishment of the Federal Reserve in particular, and the New Deal of Franklin Delano Roosevelt and its various interventions into the arrangement of property titles and money production. The first revolution occurred with the Northern invasion and its successor Reconstruction Welfare-Garrison State, in which the army was able to exert a totalitarian management of all Southern life. Abraham Lincoln waged an aggressive, brutal, and totalitarian war against a South that was composed largely of Scots-Irish yeoman, Blacks, disenfranchised Anglos, various Spanish and Mexican groups, and a plurality of Native American nations that managed to survive the Trail of Tears campaign. Lincoln, being hurled to the presidency through his demagoguery and nepotism, legislated aggressively in favor of the Northern special interest with the implementation of the Morrill Tariff (Named after Vermont steel manufacturer Justin Morrill), as well as a myriad of more protectionist measures and centralizing interventions. The largely agrarian South could not bear the weights of protectionist economic restrictions, as farmers and small property owners relied immensely on the importation of agricultural supply and machinery to maintain and increase productivity. Lincoln, however, had a special interest to keep afloat an Imperial Union that was supposed to provide wealth and power to him and his network;

---

de Sade and Marx to Hitler and Marcuse. New Rochelle, NY, Arlington House Publishers, 1974.

Lincoln was not about to let an assortment of Scots-Irish farmers, Blacks, and Mexican ranchers crush his aspirations for the American Empire. The South experienced the first wicked aspects of a culmination of modern warfare that would become prevalent throughout the 20th Century; indiscriminate involvement of the entire populace, conscription, "Blitzkrieg", and the deliberate targeting of civil improvements and non-combatants. After the onslaught of war crimes by the North, the Radical Republicans in the Imperial Capitol imposed collectivist slavery onto the South through Reconstruction; the supplanting of military generals in place of governors, the establishment of public schools to paint the Occupiers as "great liberators," and a campaign of genocide against the Plains Indians, where up to 60,000 Indians were executed by the Federal Government[18]. The growth of the American welfare-warfare State with the totalitarian occupation of the South, now has plenty of momentum with the supplanting of the libertarian tradition with statist artifice. The Progressive Era, onset in the 1880's with staggering government interventions within the Railroad industry and the Pietist conquest over the antistatist Liturgicals in culture wars, there was a drive towards an evangelical welfare provider of regulatory-statism, public schooling, central banking, and do-gooder led global hegemony. Important to discuss here as well is one of the Progressive Era's most regrettable development; the widespread legitimization of materialism and racialist pseudoscience that would lead to widespread prejudice and bigotry against Germans, Spanish/Mexicans, Italians, Poles, Irish, Blacks, Chinese, and Japanese. These false theories about racial ideals and utopias made their way throughout the university system, business, and to other leftist movements abroad; since at least the Progressive Era, a beast of sorts that shall be called "Mr. Averageman",

---

[18] "Reconstruction is typically taken to refer to the period after the War of Northern Aggression when benevolent Yankee re-educationists—sated with raping Southern women, shooting freedmen, and carrying off as much Southern property as the Federal baggage train could handle—executed a psy-ops campaign against the South." Morgan, Jason. "Reconstruction Is America's Longest War." Abbeville Institute, 2021. abbevilleinstitute.org, www.abbevilleinstitute.org/reconstruction-is-americas-longest-war.

to pay homage to E. von Kuehnelt-Leddihn, has been the backbone of the Leftist Decline. This l'homme moyen, in the terminology of Adolphe Quetelet, is mass, collective, and predictable in a social physics; his "qualities" are quantities captured by statistical metrics, in which "standard deviations" measure more or less one's averageness. Mr. Averageman is democratic man; he espouses communism, national socialism, "progressivism", social democracy, or a status quo that is logically and ideologically aligned with any one of those movements. He is skittish, fearful, and bigoted towards nonconformity; in his characteristic stupidity, learning and reasoning with those different from himself tax his materialistic comfort, and he seeks to immediately chastise or banish said "deviant." Mr. Averageman, however, acts paradoxically; in the domain of superficiality, where he thrives only, he pontificates a caricature assembled from the circular chimera of his herd; it is uberconformity. These temples of conformity are not underground, but omnipresent within the cessepit of contemporary culture; the large universities, the political institutions and their corporate cronies, act as a de facto established church of Mr. Averageman's secular faith of perfect averageness, equality, sameness. Take, for example, what Mr. Averageman peddles as education, especially in the form of standardized tests; he develops bureaucracies of number, an ecology he of course can pretend to virtue, authority, and importance. Mr. Averageman can be rewarded in a circularity in which the test (made by other Averagemen) selects for those like Mr. Averageman. He professes his "success" as indicative of right reason; but as any good Austrian knows, man is never modeled statistically or deterministcally, and what Mr. Averagemen is only capable of mustering is a superficial accumulation of number in epistemologically worthless symbolic games. Due to this, it is easy to understand Mr. Averageman's duality of unfathomable incompetence coupled with bromidial and solipsistic egotism; whenever he blunders, he is quick to blame externalities, usually represented by traditional and, almost always, Christian peoples. It is fitting, as his stupidity has sealed him off from the realm of theological existence. With naivety and general ignorance, Mr. Averageman commits himself to materialistic fallacies and proclaims, once again in circularity, that the existence of God cannot be possible because he has yet to be presented obvious, "empirical" data. His numerical reductionism is his metaphysics; he must do so, as his ecology is to match his very narrow competencies and abilities of obidence and conformity. Although not creative or intelligent enough to be scientific, he sloganeers profusely on behalf of The Science, which is none other than the aforementioned metaphysical numerical reductionism meant to serve the political religion of the Rockefeller-Morgan Empire. He clamors to charity vainly and is bitter when his trickery is exposed by both great mind and wise alike. He pathologizes those different from himself as a materialistic attempt to free himself of the burden of thought, introspection, self-critique. He is the advisor with no expertise; jaded by his failure, he refuses opportunity to those better than himself while simultaneously protesting against "oppression" from his superiors. He confides with a romanticized abstract proletariat that despises the capitalist he labors for; of course, as all things Mr. Averageman clamors so intensely to, this is not the case. He must agitates, invent this problem into existence so he can then prescribe his false pre-made solution. He occupies hollowed pulpits, once palatable due to his superiors who he has swept out. Mr. Averageman does not own a great factory, or estate, humble abode, or a true university; he "manages", as a custodian for oligarchs long since concealed from the eye, laboratories of the Prince. Garet Garrett, in his seminal essay The Revolution Was, details the harsh reality of the New Deal as a manifestation that has already passed, and nothing less than a counter-revolution is needed to take back the libertarian tradition from socialist tyranny. That is what any man of radical right must strive for; unapologetic and legitimate philosophical revolution against our enemy, the Prince, and his squire, Mr. Avengement. The Age of Enlightenment was derailed over a century ago; we live in the Age of Political Arithmetic, the Age of the Prince's Statistics, the Age of Paperwork.

About the Author

Caenan Perez is a nineteen-year-old independent philosopher and writer who has learned his disciplines through a personal library. Discovering Hans-Hermann Hoppe, Murray Rothbard, Erik von Kuehnelt-Leddihn, and Ludwig von Mises at the age of fifteen, Mr. Perez has forged a libertarian, scholastic, and continental philosophical synthesis rooted in the Catholic faith that truly distinguishes himself from the herd that has come to dominate the contemporary scene.